DIGITAL ECOSYSTEM - THE NEW ERA OF EDUCATION

DR DHEERAJ MEHROTRA

Contents

Prologue

"The best work happens when you know that it does not just work, but something that will improve other people's lives.

Satya Nadella

Preface

The book Digital Ecosystem- The New Era of Education is a priority for teachers and the education system to relate and reflect learning as a continuous process for educators and stakeholders.

Learning can't be ignored if success has to be achieved. We learn by experience and hence through experiential learning. The idea of compiling this book is to IDEATE the conception view of teaching and learning through technology as a requisite.

Dr Dheeraj Mehrotra

www.authordheerajmehrotra.com

CHAPTER ONE

THE NOVEL NORMAL IN SCHOOLS

Teaching is a priority for any teacher, but empowering is a requisite. Being an educator, a national teacher awardee, an education innovator, a KAZEN initiator in Academics, and an author, I ponder whether my learning will be updated or downgraded.

Creativity Towards Effective Classroom Management relates to new-age strategies to make an engaged learning culture with excellence within classrooms. The talk is expected to deliver an effective method to engage kids and other beneficiaries, including the parents and teachers, on the part of influential school management culture. The initiative is towards curing ignorance with the effective mechanism of implementing ORM-The Online Reputation Management and the standardised SEO- Search Engine Optimisation towards paving a sound and a WOW - Educational Climate of teaching and learning within the organisation in particular. The topic shall dwell at pace on the involvement of both

the teachers and the students in making learning happen within classrooms, particularly with the effective adoption of Technology embedded with creativity and connection among the learners in totality.

LEARNING TO LEARN, It Must be a hobby rather than an occasional occurrence. As an adult, I wish to relate the ideas one has to incorporate to be on a learning spree via the power of technology and online reputation management (ORM) as a requisite. With years of my teaching career for over 27 to count on my fingers, the most important thing I remember both as a student and a teacher is "CAN DO BETTER". This may be one of the only REMARKS or the COMMENTS in our report cards of yesteryears to mark a fun or a pun over being precise. Over the years, our learning standards have not changed, but the priority remains with a preface of the novel vocabulary of A for ANDROID, B for BLACKBERRY and C for CLOUD to taste, many.

My bucket list has had some desires, as always, with a spectrum of writing books, generating ORM- the cloud presence, and signifying Online Reputation Management has been one of my hobbies. I believe learning to learn must be a hobby rather than an occasional occurrence. The nurture of our individuality has to prioritise creating rapport with people around us as a requisite. The aim is to explore the connection and encapsulate learning via tools of one of the models of communication and excellence, NLP, popularly known as Neuro-Linguistic Programming.

There is an urgent need to emphasise implementing the concept of human excellence through our connection of Matching, Mirroring and Visualization. THE IDEA IS TO CATCH THEM YOUNG AND INNOCENT. This impacts most of our attributes and makes us wiser, more confident and dynamic. The spectrum lies in the taste of loving the subject we address and deliver with our talks and dimensions to the viewpoint in action.

Let us learn to respond and not react with the say of others, for TIME flies. Still, knowledge remains and gets credited to our nature, personality, individuality, and a means in totality. Let us learn to be flexible, innovative and willing to take risks. The sky is not always blue, and the water is not always clear; let us expand and deliver the pride to know the world with the beauty of taste to give and march smartly. The priority must be to CURE IGNORANCE and learn to matter. We as adults need to nurture the taste of being WORKING the talk and not just walking the talk or TALKING the talk as others. The pride is to make a difference by being connected.

CHAPTER TWO

TECH ADOPTION IN SCHOOLS

Teaching through technology must be a practise rather than an occasional occurrence if there has to be a Wow feature within classrooms.

As teachers, we must not use technology as a silicon coating but harness the power of technology to connect with our students. No more, it is about copying and pasting, which we have been doing over the years. Power corrupts politicians, so PowerPoint corrupts the teachers if it has just slides and no explanations. For a matter of thought and intelligence, the platform should be shared for show rather than expecting it to be the only parcel for knowledge delivery. There is a specific need to implement a new way of teaching through technology, and hence a digital pedagogy is required the most. The teachers need to introspect how children may learn in this networked environment. We can't simply take a textbook and deliver it digitally; somewhat, the need here is to explore the power to harness the best via connectivity and creativity to connect.

We can't think and re-discover the chalkboard and make it an intelligent board to deliver knowledge. What is required is a novel mindset of love, care and delivery of priorities for our children within classrooms. We ultimately need a different paradigm for teaching, a different pedagogy that talks about creation, control of chaos, connection to correcting, and consumption to creation. The teachers need to

change their thinking about how they will use technology in education.

We live in a world of change; There are great tweets each minute and great Facebook page views. The academic Donald Norman describes skeuomorphism as cultural constraints: interactions with a system learned only through culture. The time which intensifies the tech world with pride. The world has only been used in the tech industry for a few years, where its meaning has changed, says Dan O'Hara, an academic at Birmingham City University. "Skeumorphs are not strictly something that can be designed," he says. "They occur unintentionally when aesthetic styles are inherited without thinking." The photo views of Flickr, which mounts to n' undefined, explore the universal learning of repute. Each minute of over 47,000 app downloads on the apple store encapsulates a new phase of dimensional learning taking place out of the hunger for knowledge. Of course, all these facts did not exist before 2004. The availability of data online fascinates the new learner in multiple ways who tend to be a multitasker in pave to grab the unknown. To sound far-fetched but true, the schools over the years have not changed. They have taken the same task to be limited to rows and columns with a teacher at pace. They typically, at large, have no technology; hence there has been no change.

There are reports, too, "Failed iPad Experiment Shows BYOD Belongs in Schools.", "LA. Cancels iPads-in-the-schools program: a failure of vision, not technology. Despite all our heavy investments in schools, there is a failure in our strategy or the idea to implement the best technology in education. And above all, it appears to be the failure of our pedagogy. One of our mistakes as educators is CTRL + C & CTRL + V. Necessarily as COPY and PASTE for this can't solve the concerns but expands the issue in particular. This is one of the mistakes we get to govern while implementing technology in our schools.

Similarly, the conclusion fetches the scenario of apparent reasons for shifting the teaching into a new realm. The core teaching principles having a shift need an activated model to conclude without looking back in perfection. The teachers need to be an advocate for holistic education. This transforms the learners in a big way to assist learning and make it happen within the classrooms. Teachers need to keep things simple and do what works for them. For us, the teachers cannot teach the way we were taught. Above all, the students, at large, would only like the subject if they like the teacher, and this is one of the solitaire truths for any holy classroom in particular. Teachers need to have a wellness routine planning sheet, getting the win-win approach of the happiness index of the students, roll number wise. Indeed, classroom management has been identified as a primary concern for teachers, and if they don't get along with the learners as bosses or clients with affection, the management of the class appears slang. The teachers in the majority have a wrong notion that classroom management is much to do with discipline only and is limited to the children being quiet in the class.

In contrast, the goals include identifying misconceptions about managing the teaching, the students and the consequences. The teachers of age need to broaden the very conception of classroom management and ultimately provide a framework among their

colleagues for developing their classroom management plan. Engaging the children in instructions often leads to classroom management but is limited to a classic time only. There has to be a thoughtful physical environment for an activated classroom supported by establishing caring relationships and implementing engaging instructions.

CHAPTER THREE

Achieving a Student-Driven Classroom

The learning has taken its pace to the majority who, by chance or tribes, are governed by today's Google Generation. Alas, to the say, the teachers are no longer the fountain of knowledge but artistic adults to manage the classroom discipline.

The teachers who motivate, differentiate, make content relevant and leave no student behind are more important than any other factor. Students like the subject only when they like the teacher, hence a directly proportional element within a classroom. The drive by the teacher in the class with the vocabulary is signified by the equilibrium of learning together rather than teaching. They say, "Teachers know the best", which activates wisdom just in the franchise but in action. The sole reason for this far-fetched approach lies in the nutshell element of a straightforward process of open knowledge, which is unrestricted, versatile and dual with surprises. The satisfaction and the wow part within classrooms only prevail where there is a taste of "It is in the book, Ma'am, tell us something new!" As a teacher, it is our wisdom to teach the "I can do approach" instead of the "I shall try approach", which is universally possible only when we use kind words in the class. Compliment each kid, especially the difficult ones. That might be the only positive thing they hear all day.

Activating a student-oriented rather than a task-oriented classroom requires more of a connection, a relationship with the student. At times apologising to students is a learning moment. If we want kids with character, we must model it to them with others, as character counts. The experiences shared in totality that a genuine apology requires freely admitting fault, fully accepting responsibility, a humbled asking for forgiveness, immediately changing the behaviour, and actively rebuilding the trust. The dose of willingness to explore knowledge is what is desired rather than sharing contents from the book. When students appear crusaders of expertise, the teachers need to act like a facilitator more but strict disciplinarian in particular. It must be made clear to everyone that there is no expiry date for hunger for learning. Let yearning for knowledge be a priority rather than an occasional occurrence. Also, the teachers must explore the power of curing ignorance as to the chief element of choice in every interaction with the students, teachers, peers and parents. It is never too late to make yourself better; it should be the priority. The segment of reality lies in engaging the children in the class with no fear but intimacy and a feeling of pride both by the students and the teachers. To the real concerns, the fear kills the dreams more than failure ever will, which should be mounted on priority by the masses. The children should be made to enjoy the classroom session with engagement and knowledge sharing using ICT tools and techniques of the cyber world and making their Online reputation management a reality.

Today's students are no longer kids but young adults and hence need recognition as individuals and partners in the learning process. Critical thinking must be one of the prime qualities of the children as it is among the first causes for change, but is a parish in schools- for no other reason than it conditions the mind to suspect the form and function of everything it sees, including the classroom scenario, all what is taught and discussed. As a teacher, it is our prime requisites to make progress visible, adjust grading practices, model desired habits and don't get carried away with the politics of the school, the students and the parents. Hey, the voice violates, the Principal's lobby is rushed for, is there any debating subject rises or fumes up. The school principal is targeted and reassured support to the students, as ever be.

To govern and sense student's friendly classroom, the teachers need to check on their share of the day, of some new vocabulary and make a haze to the fact that the students should be held accountable for the number and the quality of questions students ask and pursue during the teaching-learning process. From Good Morning Wishing to the, Thank you, children, the time and share has to be so friendly and empowering to make them take home moments of joy and some attributes to share with their parents. This must be a priority. Teachers need to showcase in action that they are not perfect and never will be. They must take risks with their teaching, and failing must be a part of the learning process. We face the Google Generation, which empowers self and is not dependent on either the library or the teacher; fortunately, I doubt my words too.

The beautiful words help our children use a wide range of captivating words in their writings. We must not blame them for their handwriting and knowledge limitations; instead, they must be the part and the parcel of their learning. Also, to create a rapport with the students, the teaching tools in practice by the teachers need to be evaluated concerning whether the usage during the lesson is appropriate. With this, the teacher's subject knowledge, enthusiasm, questioning methods, exposition, and problem-solving related to the multilevel dimension for judging. The teachers as facilitators explore and expose the learning objectives in a big bang way via repartees and the responses generated after every class or via the Parents' Teachers' Meetings on jolt and achievements. Let us conclude the fact that children will love and explore their presence in the classrooms only when given the recognition of individual concerns; teachers must call the kids by their first names keeping them at pace to importance rather than experiencing the only preface with them at the time of the roll calls and that too with referencing through roll numbers.

The choice is ours, engage or enrage! Let quality be the taste forever instead of being just an occasional occurrence. The priority must be to create a WOW classroom with the tongue of "You can do wonders", "You can do it!" and above all ", All my students are the best of the students, and I am proud of them".

CHAPTER FOUR

The Engaged Teaching

Ma'am, please tell us something new! This is already in the book. Comes the reply to any subject related interactions today in today's classrooms. To the surprise of many, the Walls and Friend Requests have come across as more popular than HELLO or Hi!

Are we on the same page? The choice is ours to intercept the juncture regarding making the best of job operations, delivering the best with pride and honour and above all, meeting standards the requisite for the schools to flourish. The marketing mantras sponsor the best the teachers' satisfaction but in a new role of cyber presence now. The need for today towards the teaching segment has dwelled with intelligence and IT-friendly requisites by all. Quality Education is reflected by the involvement of the quality infrastructure in the learning arena, which otherwise is not of any use and Children Friendly.

The parents are requested to make their choices today for admission in the majority of the mushrooming shops around the country more like any other service industry with the option to have around the school, the classes and even they are told to leave their wards in the class as a trial run for them to decide of taste. Computers, software, CDs and Smart Toys ought to be considered as a supplement to the other, more concrete learning activities like completing puzzles, building with LEGO and blocks, reading books, creating art projects and playing on the playground...", is evident by our observations and research, out of the present-day scenario. On very grounds of improvement planning and the paradigm shift with education being characterised by technology-enabled instructions, collaborative learning, multidisciplinary problem-solving and promoting critical thinking skills, e-learning, a household name for the students today, offers a wide variety of ICT enabled classroom solutions for learning the Smart Way! It allows a user-friendly option for the learner to integrate what is desired and acquired to their requirements class and level wise.

'No talking boys and girls can no longer be the most common vocabulary for the teachers for the new learner demands and explores the power of engagement within the classrooms and that of the narration to examine the

connection via the cyber world with the teachers in reality. No wonder you tell a child to write an essay as homework; they are bound to download the content to present before you the next day, making you baffled by the interest of the many others lying in the queue. The parents often think of this as a menace out of the challenging work wisdom they possess to earn their daily living. Their frames are not yet over with more demands for the CD-Burner and Scanner for more computing and smart-study, as they call it. The only option available to the poor parents of the IT age is to ponder over for solace and accept novel ways to convince their future generations regarding motivations and guided involvement.

The TEACHERS need to harness the requirements to the best of their abilities and interest further. They need to depend on some SMART teaching options available to them in the classroom to make the learning scenario enjoyable to the kids. This offers an innovative methodology to educate every child of the country with specialisation in the art of scalability involving people, processes and technology—the focus applicants towards building the innovative capabilities and performance at the institutional level periodically.

We have DIGITALLY ORIENTED CLASSROOMS now in every school, but does that solve the purpose? I doubt my experience. It is the teachers' mindset that the educators need to function well. The Teacher ought to be a TRAINER/ LEARNER/ ALL ROUNDER, with their presence in the CYBERSPACE mandatory. No longer having an EMAIL ID and expertise of MS OFFICE but more and more...viz....having a WEBSITE, BLOG, WiKi, and more, apart from being SOCIALLY NETWORKED 24x7. Also, we need to remember that Teachers become enamoured with YouTube, TED, and WatchKnowLearn or any Ready Reckoner Web Content of interest with Quality and Cream!

But at the same time, it is indispensably true to keep in mind. However, computer software cannot teach a child the concepts they are not developmentally ready for. Computers should always be considered a supplement to other, more concrete learning activities like completing puzzles, building with Lego and blocks, reading books, creating art projects and playing on the playground. Keeping the database analysis in view out of the day is universally true.

Various researchers and scholars have defined the need for Quality Education. Still, no one has ever desired the lack of "We", the teachers today, to be exciting and "Informed" with the march of time, or else we would be the only "Un-interested" thing (Identity) in the class if we are not enriching and of any interest to the children to make them forget their Facebook Walls' and the SMS which otherwise make their mind fertile of interest.

The use of technology not only makes the entire process of learning exciting but more impactful as well. Unfortunately, the education sector has always held a reputation of being a laggard as far as technology adoption goes. There must be a mindset toward the Think Tank, and decision-making must occur. I do recall circular No. 57, dt. 01.09.2010 by the Central Board of Secondary Education, to all the heads of institutions affiliated with the board, which says that the 21st century is characterised by the emergence of a knowledge-based society wherein Information and Communication Technology play a pivotal role. The convergence of computer, communication and content technologies, being known as ICT, has attracted the attention of academia, business, government and communities to use it for innovating profitable propositions. ICT has permeated every walk of life, affecting fields such as launching satellites, managing business across the globe, and enabling social networking. It is becoming simpler to use desktop palms top, iPods, iPad etc. The truth is that Students are closer to Technology than we are, especially the Hand-Held Devices or the Ubiquitous resources. Their comprehension of these resources is exponential, which you will discover only as you get close to them.

With the utility segments available to the trio, the teachers, parents, and students exploring the innovative Education delivery products, there is a particular belief that low-cost information and communication technology tools are empowering the way of change. As a result, students and workers require new skills and innovative abilities in their learning, livelihood, and life. For meaningful and purposeful education, there is an urgent need for the schools to function as a learning hub for the entire community and be equipped with all the facilities as per the community's needs. Similarly, the district has to extend their cooperation to the schools for the child's holistic development. Hence, there is an urgent need to cooperate and collaborate between all society stakeholders. The school makes the community and the country thereby. The National Policy on ICT in School Education by MHRD Govt. of India states, "The ICT policy in School Education aims at preparing youth to participate creatively in the establishment, sustenance and growth of a knowledge society leading to the all-around social-economic development of the nation and global competitiveness". Here is the solution, a must for all schools to practice Quality Education with a flare of interest generating learning environments.

CHAPTER FIVE

Augmented Reality in Schools

In a layman's voice, the 'Augmented Reality' is a concept which combines the real and the virtual, giving people a view of reality which has been tweaked, enhanced or augmented. The utility is with the usage of smartphones. The delivery of digital learning at pace in today's classrooms has paved a reverberating demand to explore anything of innovation and desire to generate a WOW- Wonder of Wonders within today's classrooms.

The Evaluation of AR:

Although augmented reality may seem like the stuff of science fiction, researchers have been building a prototype system for more than three decades. The first was developed in the 1960s by computer graphics pioneer Ivan Sutherland and his students at Harvard University. In the 1970s and 1980s, many researchers studied augmented reality at an institution such as the U.S. Air Force's Armstrong Laboratory, the NASA Ames Research Center and the University of North Carolina at Chapel Hill. It wasn't until the early 1990s that the term "Augmented Reality "was coined by scientists at Boeing who were developing an experimental AR system to help workers assemble wiring harnesses. In 1996 developers at Columbia University developed 'The Touring Machine'. In 2001 MIT came up with a very compact AR system known as "MIThrill". Presently, research is developing BARS (Battlefield Augmented Reality Systems) by engineers at Naval Research Laboratory, Washington D.C. Of late, the revolution has paved over software scores to supplement AR in action.

The showcases and roadshows are clubbed in conjunction with AR to make the same an event of fun, frolic and participatory. The simple sound byte with a video can be shared at the youtube presence of the Mahindra XUV500 Augmented Reality at Auto Expo 2012 at http://www.youtube.com/

watch?v=iA-2ElU9Qs8. It rightly justifies that Augmented Reality (AR) is a term for a live direct or indirect view of a physical, real-world environment whose elements are augmented by computer-generated sensory input, such as sound or graphics.

What some may call an 'unsurprising' 71% of 16 to 24-years-olds own smartphones, so why aren't teachers utilising these in the classroom or on campus? AR shouldn't be another monster under the bed (or desk), says Judy Bloxham – used intelligently, it provides new ways for learners to access content and knowledge.

The time demands, and so does the scenario. Is the use of these devices going to detract from the learning process or contribute to future workplace skills? Should teachers be using augmented reality (AR) techniques to engage students and develop their skills for the modern world? Well, I say 'yes', quotes: Bloxham.

The beauty lies in the output which is generated. As per the researchers, AR allows people to add digital content to printed material, geographic locations and objects. Then using a smart device or tablet, viewers can scan a thing, and the digital content will appear. The digital information can range from a link to a website, an invitation to make a phone call, a video, a 3D model, or any other supported digital information.

The knowledge base pokes of the co-existence of this practice with the march of time. AR provides a more effective way to enable learners to access the content. A 'QR code' is simply a shortcut to a URL – it has no other meaning in its own right. Many AR platforms use a visual browser to recognise an image. There is no need to add a special symbol to trigger the content.

CHAPTER SIX

The Digital Teaching

Cyber based computing has evolved into a new era of learning thy way ! !! via cyberspace at the pace of your own and no definition of the

classroom restricted with the four walls of the classroom to be severe and private. Teachers who once were the SAGE on the STAGE are now forced to be the guides on the floor. They act like facilitators now to students as an aid to learning which is now more of a formality in classrooms. Most of the time, he is told the same things that have been already shared with him by their parents/ friends or at the online tutorial option through the various search engines, primarily the GOOGLE. We encapsulate the very nature of learning, but with a bit of intelligence; otherwise, they come up to us (probably if not, will with the march of time and tide); I quote, "Sir/ Madam, It is already in the book. Please tell us something new". Do we have a reply to them?

Various researchers and scholars have defined the need for Quality Education. Still, no one has ever desired the lack of "We", the teachers today, to be exciting and "Informed" with the march of time, or else we would be the only "Un-interested" thing (Identity) in the class if we are not enriching and of any interest to the children to make them forget their Facebook Walls' and the SMS which otherwise make their mind fertile of interest.

The branching of tabs in the classrooms has delivered a new preface of learning, with teachers discovering information and sharing it verbatim. Over the years, with the march of time and tide, the education system has delivered progress to the nation and the world as all Top companies globally pay attention and work on the rolls of Indians known for their Expertise and Intelligence.

The delivery of new order learning for our children explores the intelligence with teachers in demand of being a ROCKSTAR. The application of novel modules integrated with multimedia based packages/ contents applicate to the new learning for our 21st Century Googlers. The Indian Scenario of the Academic climate of schools has had a remarkable sense of change and modularity through the introduction of CCE. It has been rightly nurtured via the Mentor/ Mentee research-based delivery by the Central Board of Secondary Education. What I believe, in a sense, is the change which needs to be mustered. We must think that Learning should be just that, not memorisation of content provided by the instructor, which limits people who have different learning styles (auditory, visual, kinesthetic etc.) to assimilate the information. Above all, the Indian learning scenario needs to be focused on an outcome, not THE outcome of the result allowing for different perspectives of thought and internalisation of the subject. The collaborative *model takes it one step further, which incorporates a team on a "hunt" for information forming a conclusion based on personal land shared perspective (synthetic learning) highly desired today.*

The promotion in the case of implementing the new tools of learning has yielded in generating the Quality cult in schools of today with a spectrum of inputs through the stakeholders viz. Parents, Students and the teachers. Indeed, the teachers are no longer the sole imparters of knowledge. Still, they need to empower the students to learn at a pace and their leisure through personal learning networks keeping their unique traits of talents and interests. The teachers don't end after the class is over but on the jolt for 24 hours around the cyber linkage or other social networks. There is no wall now or the boundary of learning. The innovative educator has to evolve a personal learning network for improvement first. Not only this, she has to reach the students where there is no boundary or limitation in a big way. It is a way to build one's own classroom and network of learning. The change or the shift here is that we can connect and share ideas which are not so in the one to many modes of classroom learning.

They must be given an opportunity only when required but as a habit to my knowledge and interest. The module, particularly by Next Education India, delivers TeachNext, one of the highly enriched packed e-learning delivery, and is entitled to successful learning. With over 6,000 schools, the product provides e-learning with perfection and common interest to the pupils with pride!

The innovative learning is not limited to a physical space but an open learning scenario with a preface to one's comfort in his reading home at home or a TV room at large. It is very much unlike the classroom learning with the same group all day, all the time. Here the community is different, and the learning is more spectacular further. Here the teacher concerned is the one who has to be engaged and involved in the conversations as a leader or a facilitator further. And this makes the Indian Education System more challenging to face the 21st Century Learners...who are fertile already with knowledge and come to classrooms to route their intelligence and explore collaborative learning and a Win-Win exploration of situations at times.

Kudos to the Teachers who are challenged at all times with students arguing about their favourite replies or responses to their queries in the classrooms. Hopefully, the e-learning or the digital classes help the learning teachers to a limit.

Any comments..! Are we prepared. . . Sounds exciting, and we need to prepare for the showcase if we want patient learning to occur in our classrooms.

CHAPTER SEVEN

INNOVATIVE EDUCATORS OF PRIME IMPORTANCE

A Teacher, who is now a facilitator in this generation, encapsulates a new order of delivery with the extension of a knowledge society and not a content delivery or an interpretation of book knowledge in real life. The innovation is the ultimate to generate interest in learning for the kids today. It mounts a lot of energy and thoughts to be an innovative educator who is of particular requisite to deliver the knowledge to today's cyber society.

The mantra is Engage Me or Enrage Me, from the side of the students at large.

Indeed, the teachers are no longer the sole imparters of knowledge. Still, they need to empower the students to learn at a pace and their leisure through personal learning networks keeping their unique traits of talents and interests. The teachers don't end after the class is over but on the jolt for 24 hours around the cyber linkage or other social networks. There is no wall now or the boundary of learning. The innovative educator has to evolve a personal learning network for improvement first. It has to reach the students as well where there is no boundary or limitation in a big way. It is a way to build one's own classroom and network of learning. The change or the shift here is that we can connect and share ideas which are not so in the one to many modes of classroom learning.

The fact lies in the teacher being an innovator of traits and essence to explore the attention in the classroom. The priority of taking Education and technology to go together laminates with the questions in our minds, viz. Should we do more or less? What about virtual schools? Interactive whiteboards? Smartphones? Facebook and Twitter? Should kids be using the internet? Should kids choose what they learn on the internet? These are legitimate conversations, and each person has to make these kinds of decisions based on their comfort levels and individual student needs.

The 21st-century innovative learning is not limited to a physical space but an open learning scenario with a preface to one's comfort in his reading home or a TV room at large. It is very much unlike the classroom learning with the same group all day, all the time. Here the community is different, and the learning is more spectacular further. Here the teacher concerned is the one who has to be engaged and involved in the conversations as a leader or a facilitator further.

As per the demands and research, the challenge is to create an integrated education system that:

Provides access to quality education that is practical, relevant, customised and effective.

Can adopt tech-based innovative ways to provide faster expansion of educational opportunities to all.

Looks for bridging the gap between education and employability.

Promotes social equality/economic viability.

One policy is not going to help all. The need of the hour is to have specific guidelines for various levels and areas of education specific to multiple regions.
As an academician, I feel that "Everyone is a genius. But if you judge a fish by its ability to climb a tree, it will live its whole life believing that it is stupid." as do one of the inventors of past years.

CHAPTER EIGHT

Mindfulness Within Classrooms

The priority talks about reality and maturity through technology.

It is assumed that mindfulness is only beneficial for adults as only adults feel stressed. But it is quite the contrary. Children can be affected by stress, too, especially in academic focus. Students experience toxic stress every day thanks to the pressures of getting good grades, the increasingly competitive environment, and the uncertainty of the future.

Today, it has become widespread to hear Class III students feel miserable only because they failed to understand a particular subject or got bad grades in an exam. Teaching mindfulness in school at a very impressionable age is essential. It is an important method to help young students cope with stress and achieve excellence in learning.

Improves Attention and Cognitive Skills

One of the biggest reasons students can't focus in class is because of a low attention span. Even those who are toppers can lose focus every once in a while. This often leaves students feeling bad about themselves.

Mindfulness and meditation can solve this problem as it directly affects the brain, especially the hippocampus associated with memory, particularly long-term memory. Practising mindfulness can help the students concentrate better. And since it jogs the hippocampus to be more active, their memory and critical learning skills will improve and help them get better grades.

Develops Better Interpersonal Skill

The competition and the pressure to always be the best can affect a student's social and emotional well-being. They tend to focus on themselves and do not care about their surroundings.

Having good interpersonal skills is very important. It is the means to survive in the real world. Educational institutions must ensure that the pressure to perform does not harm a child's interpersonal skills. Mindfulness training will also make the prefrontal cortex, the part of the brain that regulates emotion, more active. As a result, students will become more empathetic and friendly and improve their behaviour in school.

Helps Cope With Stress

Stress is not a stranger in our life, and it is also very typical for students to experience stress. However, the challenges of the modern education system often force students to experience stress that can negatively affect their mental health.

It is a sad truth, but as adults, many students do not know how to deal with their stress. This can prove to be quite dangerous. It can lead to various problems from an inability to regulate mood, impaired attention, even physical problems and depression.

School should not only focus on lessons and grades but also on education for life. Our education system should pay attention to the students' well too, and mindfulness meditation is one of the best methods. It can teach the students to improve their mindful awareness, help them cope with stress, enhance optimism about life, and improve their school performance.

CHAPTER NINE

Tech Preparedness in VUCA World

As an educator, I feel with the COVID era and post the same, Learning to learn as a priority has to have dwelled with the practice for a notion to commit to quality in academics. We as educators realise that Learning how to learn is a game-changer in the global knowledge spectrum, and it's never too early or, in fact, too late to teach students how to begin to learn more independently.

We stand to harness the roots of learning with innovation and creativity with the march of time. After a couple of years of remote and hybrid instruction, many students and teachers have become accomplished technology users and curators of knowledge, which has even resulted in leveraging sophisticated tech tools to facilitate learning both in and out of the classroom. No more is the learning limited within the classrooms of the four walls, in particular. But like any area of expertise, there are always innovative ways to sharpen skills, streamline workloads, and increase access to and via technology in a big bang way!

My belief as an educator goes with being an independent learner, post covid as a priority for kids and the educators in future. Assist them in affirming their commitment to organise themselves, manage their focus over time, and limit distractions.

VUCA is an abbreviation that arose out of the military during the 1990s. It portrays the "haze of war" — the turbulent conditions experienced in an advanced combat zone. Its importance to pioneers in business is evident, as these conditions elucidate the climate where the company is led each day. Authority, not surprisingly, including making a dream, isn't sufficient in a VUCA world. TEACHING IN THE VUCA WORLD, a card priority fetches the world of uncertainties. The new world order of VOLATILE, UNCERTAIN, COMPLEX, and AMBIGUOUS approaches reflect a new everyday learning and exploring the novel order of working.

- *Volatile: Things change eccentrically, out of nowhere, very, particularly for the more regrettable.*

- *Uncertain: Important data isn't known or clear; suspicious, hazy about the current circumstance and future results; not ready to be depended upon.*

- *Complex: Many unique and associated parts: key choice factors, the connection between assorted specialists, development, variation, coevolution, feeble signs.*

- *Ambiguous: Open to more than one translation; the significance of an occasion can be perceived unexpectedly.*

Driving in a VUCA world not just gives a moving climate to pioneers to work and for chief advancement program to have an effect: it likewise gives an essential scope of new abilities. The new truth is acknowledging that new and various skills are required for pioneers to prevail in this new typical.

As educators, we need to guide our students and parents towards new destinations, which may include:

Flourish amid unpredictability, vulnerability, intricacy and equivocalness.

Recognise the need to choose what you centre around

Construct an essential organisation of essential contacts

Realise were to work at your pinnacle

Output your frame of reference for changes, patterns, dangers and openings

Bridle the basic achievement framework for life during the transition; the Powerhouse Loop

The Online Teaching and Learning with the Parents Support

Well, finally, to explore the wonders amongst the PANDEMIC and the readiness to the VUCA world, without a doubt, the word VUCA causes some cocked eyebrows. It characterises the prepared idea of shock, an evoke stun, shock, or offence, ordinarily through whimsical activities or talks. The expression regularly recommends negative consideration or judgment. However, my dear companions serve a reality today.

As ahead of a school me, I discovered checking and testing quickly of solace for the educators to be locked in and module to the learning situation. The range deceives our arrangement which screens. Thus, training has changed drastically with the unmistakable ascent of e-learning, whereby education is attempted distantly and in advanced stages. The paging is organised and characterised by the characteristic of conveying the classes without any difficulty and solace to their takers.

The target of this module enacts learning concerning the Leading Change in a Pandemic

VUCA World specifically. The shared vision and methodology characterise the destinations with the introduction of understanding the idea of visualising the learning. It incorporates the model to deal with the world through VOCA in the COVID period. Step by step instructions to prepare pioneers to oversee through. The idea represents Volatility, Uncertainty, Complexity, and Ambiguity, as VOCA practically speaking.

CHAPTER TEN

CONCLUSION

As we know, learning online has become a more significant challenge for our kids in reality. The experts predict that the results will affect the learning outcome in years to come. We as educators are making a lot of effort to make learning visible, but we need a new model implementation. The interest to learn and teach post-pandemics has prompted valuable connections in people, advancements, societies, and enterprises. At the centre of instructing and learning necessities lies a requirement for curiosity and interest in improvement. Teaching is no such a place where there is no change at all. The whole teaching and learning platform have changed. The lethal pandemic has constrained humankind to advance and foster better approaches for bestowing instruction to understudies of all ages. Nobody will go to school except for everybody who is learning. Advancement has significantly changed how understudies are learning, and

educators are instructing. The development has overhauled everybody's perspectives about the world out there.

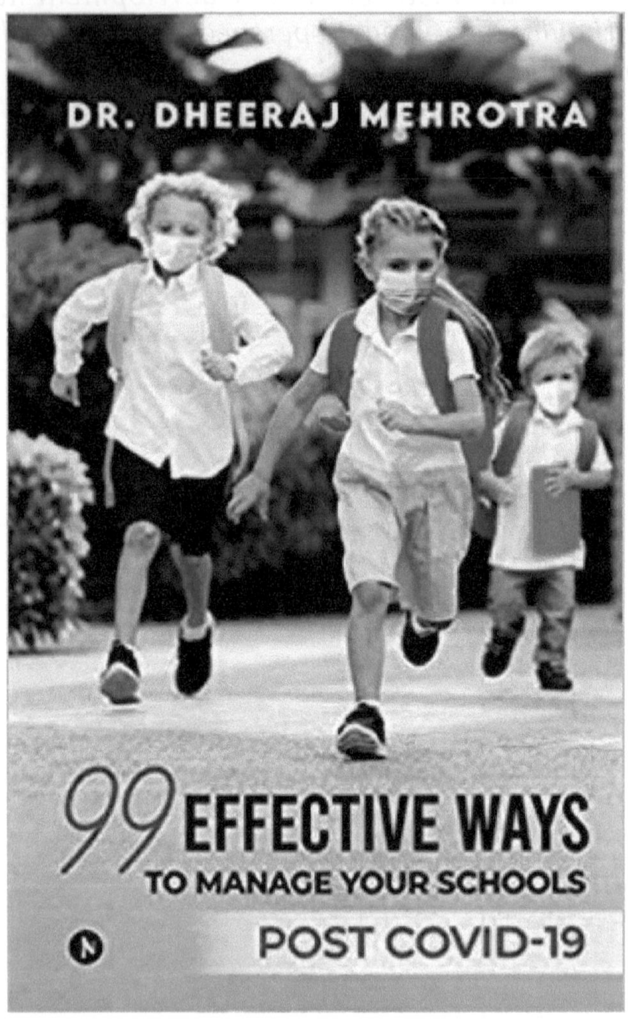

Available at AMAZON!

In the current period, the web is viewed as significantly heavenly. In contrast to a pen or furrow, it doesn't have a place with, nor is it solely utilised by its proprietor. The worldwide scenario employs it, and educators have acquired a more extensive effort with its assistance. During the startling disturbance of Covid-19, when individuals were shaken out of safe places, confusing things occurred in the advanced world. The change was taken well and adopted to the mechanism at pace. The closure of schools has made learning not at all speed but an optional attribute in reality. It is now with the comfort of the home, the personal interest and the engagement, which vary from student to student.

Notwithstanding the lockdown requirements, educators have become more firmly associated around the world and locally - on account of the magic of computerised innovations. More individuals can learn more subjects of their decision on the web, without hardly lifting a finger and opportunity, than previously. Educators from one side of the planet to the other have never been as interconnected, reliant, and intelligent as they are currently. Notwithstanding the recognisable domain of actual communications, computerised advances have talented instructors. Another space of virtual exercise conveyance stretched to the vast majority. Online teaching and learning have created a lot of challenges. Managing the education for kids is a task to be evaluated now. Web-based showing presence hasn't been full-fledged and is going through progress. Robert Moore composes suitably, "In all types of distance educating, the capacity to adapt the relationship with far off students is significant." Following are a few things that educators can improve on the online stage as a part of the new age of learning and delivering the teaching. These reflect the learning preface and allocate education as a priority in particular.

Gathering criticism and recovering from the same:

Educators should gather online education as a priority and, at the same time, look for its' criticism to distinguish what is and isn't working. The assessment of online teaching trends matters and ought to be offered influence to work on web-based learning. This will persuade the online teaching with the emphasis that the educator is intrigued and put resources into every understudy. Students shouldn't feel that they are drawing with a Personal Computer. That may usually be an inclination of disconnectedness in web-based learning. They ought to be pulling in with one another, the educator, and the substance.

Show matters for the Students and Parents

As likely interruptions encircle the home climate, keeping understudies connected with and propelled in their exercises is probably the most outstanding test instructors face while educating on the web. The show is vital to cause the understudies to feel about the newness of the climate. Instructors should be pleasantly spruced up alongside clean areas and have more coordinated conversations. On the off chance that understudies can see your face, it will be more spurring for them if you look drawn in and take interest with virtuous tolerance. Enlightening slide shows and recordings ought to have a decent picture quality.

The Instructors who educate in a similar tone can frequently make understudies feel exhausted and detached. Changing the manner of speaking to present new exercises or stirring up the rhythm can have constructive outcomes. Educators can work on narrating abilities and applause for all to hear. A solid web association with the coordinated substance before each class is likewise essential to working on the interest of understudies. The cloud connect is hence the responsibility of all the educators on priority. The concept of ORM- Online Reputation Management is hence a requisite.

Utilising innovation as a Priority

How should I teach? How to connect well with the students? All matters in the online spectrum and also in the actual classrooms. A broad scope of online devices, for example, whiteboards, printers, virtual games, content managers, drawing devices, record editors, breakout rooms, or screen sharing devices, can likewise cause understudies to remain alert. Examinations and allures can again have extraordinary positive outcomes. Turning up music or simply playing with various apparatuses can keep understudies quiet.

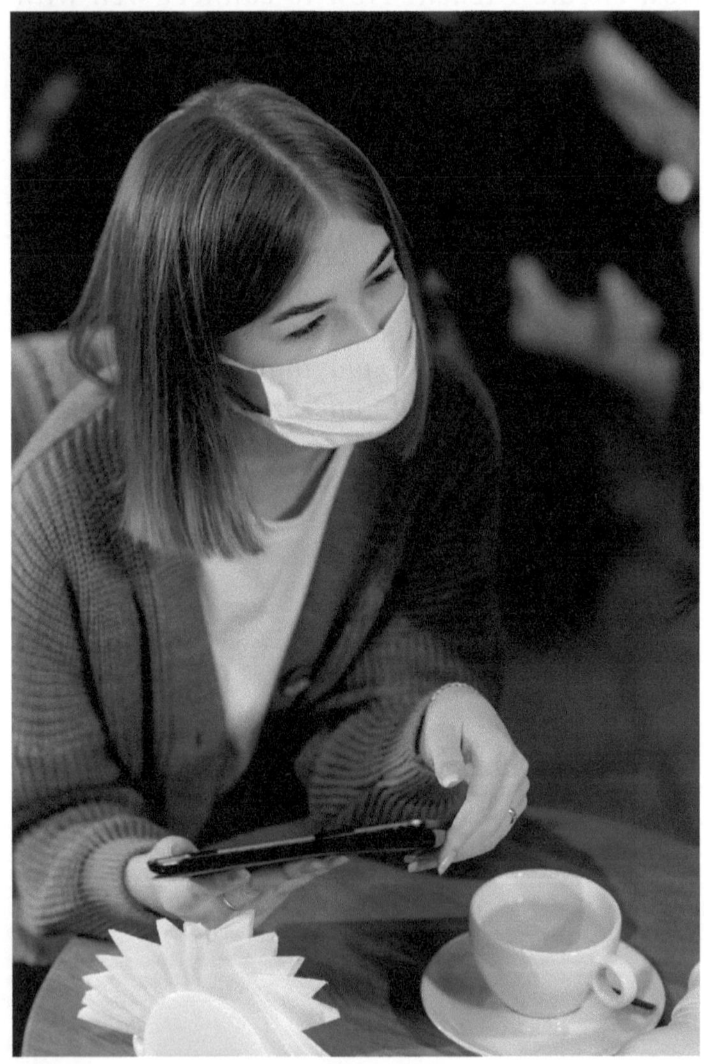

Defining objectives for a better learning outcome

The objectives as a takeaway, the objective as delivery and the learning outcome by the children all reflect an identity to explore learning in particular. Another approach to help the teaching methodology that remains focused on their online examinations or assessment is also required to cater to the defined objectives. Such a mechanism aids in helping them to remember their advancement. One straightforward approach to bringing transient dreams into the online study hall is to ensure every exercise has a clear layout that an instructor imparts to her understudies. Hence, they know where they are in the learning cycle and the setting for any movement they are doing. This will help the students to self-assess their advancement.

Regarding long-haul objectives, going excessively far into the future probably won't be powerful. Yet, instructors should have a go at setting aside time once in a while to check in with the understudies and put forward objectives together for the following month. As educators, we have to follow the spectrum with the new angle of teaching and learning. Here engaging the kids works wonders. It has to be part and parcel of every online classroom on priority.

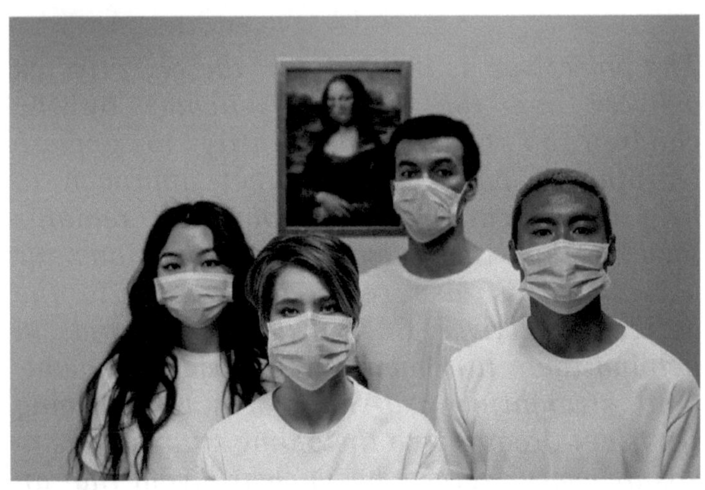

Keeping a connection with the environment

The educator's identity has changed with the march of the CORONA, and now it is like learning to learn as a new preface. We as educators need to explore the identity of more than just being the teacher but a learner. In a vis-à-vis class, it's run of the mill to give understudies some quiet reflection time to work alone or read content as extensive exercises don't interpret well in online homerooms. Long, thick messages are trying to peruse on a screen or the mobile tablets. Thus, quietness doesn't solve that well in virtual homerooms as it gives the ideal pardon to an understudy's regard for float somewhere else. Hence, arranging exercises that keep understudies effectively clicking, composing, or talking through the training is the best approach for educators. Instructors can do this by posing heaps of inquiries, including games, and ensuring students need to do things like using attracting apparatuses or typing the discourse boxes. From monitoring to giving instructions, assuring assignments all reflect at ease for the needful. We very well know that the pandemic has modelled the classroom learning to a new phase; a life without education for all the girls and boys is a life without any rights. While school closures are an effective precautionary measure to contain the spread of COVID-19, evidence from previous emergencies suggests that the longer children are unable to attend learning facilities, the more likely they will never return to school. This is a grave concern for all we, the educators today!

About The Author

Dheeraj Mehrotra, MS, MPhil, PhD (Education Management) honoris causa., a white and a yellow belt in SIX SIGMA, a Certified NLP Business Diploma holder, is an Educational Innovator, Author, with expertise in Six Sigma In Education, Academic Audits, Neuro-Linguistic Programming (NLP), Total Quality Management In Education, an Experiential Educator, a CBSE Resource towards School Assessment (SQAA), CCE, JIT, Five S, and KAIZEN. He has authored over 40 books on Computer Science for ICSE/ ISC/ CBSE Students, over 60 books of academic interest for the field of education excellence, and Six Sigma. A former Principal at De Indian Public School, New Delhi, (INDIA) with an ample teaching experience of over Two Decades, he is a certified Trainer for Quality Circles/ TQM in Education and QCI Standards for School Accreditation/ Six Sigma in Education.

He has also been honoured with the President of India's National Teacher Award in the year 2006 and the Best Science Teacher State Award (By the Ministry of Science and Technology, State of UP), Innovation in Education for his inception of Six Sigma In Education by Education Watch, New Delhi and Education World- Best Teacher Award, BOLT Learner Teacher Award by Air India, 'Innovation in Education Award 2016' by Higher Education Forum (HEF), Gujarat Chapter, among others.

He has developed over 150 FREE EDUCATIONAL MOBILE Apps for the Google Play Store exclusively for Teachers, Students, and Parents. This work has been recognised by the LIMCA BOOK OF RECORDS & INDIA BOOK OF RECORDS as the only Indian to draw that feast. Dr Mehrotra is presently working as a PRINCIPAL at KUNWARS GLOBAL SCHOOL, Lucknow, in India. He has conducted over 1000 workshops globally on "Excellence In Education" integrated with Total Quality Management and Six Sigma, Technology Integration in Education (TIE), Developing towards being ROCKSTAR TEACHERS, including Cyberspace, Cyber Security, Classroom Management, School Leadership & Management, and Innovative teaching within classrooms via Mind Maps, NLP and Experiential Learning in Academics. He is an active TEDx speaker and can be viewed on the youtube TEDx channel.

As a premium UDEMY Instructor, he has also developed over 450 courses and is catering to over 8 Lakh students from 180 plus countries.

He can be visited at www.authordheerajmehrotra.com.

ABOUT THE AUTHOR

Books By The Same Author

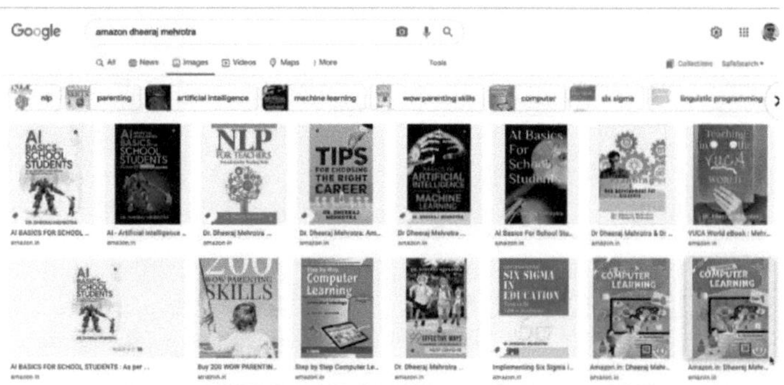

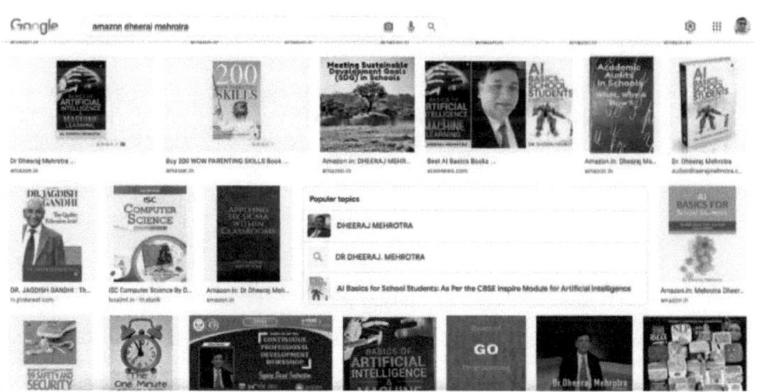

9 798886 847550

Printed by Libri Plureos GmbH in Hamburg, Germany